Cybersecurity: The Nation's Greatest Threat To Critical Infrastructure

Cyber threat is one of the most serious economic and national security challenges we face as a nation.

—President Barrack Obama[1]

The National Cyber Security Framework Manual of 2012 estimates that in a decade, the Internet will touch 60% of the world's population (over five billion citizens); will interlink more than 50 billion physical objects and devices, and will contribute to at least 10% of developing nations' Gross Domestic Product (GDP).[2] The velocity, functionality, and openness of the Internet drive innovation, and enable and empower everything in the nation from vast social networks, the financial services industry, the military industrial complex, defense, government and emergency services networks, and critical national and global infrastructure. Pervasive dependency on the Internet, and a diffuse spectrum of threats and vulnerabilities, compounded with irresolute and inconsistent leadership, policy and command and control concerning cyber critical infrastructure protection[3] create the potential for catastrophic cyber incident on a scale comparable to Hurricane Katrina in 2005."[4] An accident, attack, or natural disaster could drastically affect infrastructure critical to public safety, and national or economic security, and devastate the lives of Americans or to the security of the Nation itself.[5]

In 2012, President Obama identified cybersecurity as one of the most serious economic and national security challenges that the Nation faces.[6] U.S. critical infrastructure sectors provide the foundation for security, governance, economic vitality, and the American way of life.[7] Currently, the United States lacks an integrated national cybersecurity strategy, that even at the strict behest of the President, the bipartisan government has yet to construct, approve or effectively implement to protect critical infrastructure. Complicating the issue, Department of Defense (DOD), Department of Homeland Security (DHS), United States Cyber Command (USCYBERCOM), a diffuse array of government agencies, and the private business sector share the responsibilities for cybersecurity protection of national critical infrastructure. Additionally, DHS, responsible for the complex mission of Homeland Defense, maintains responsibility for private sector network protection. The private sector owns and manages 85 - 90% of the critical infrastructure.[8] Legislatively, DSH has no authority to protect private networks. Over the past decade, the cyber threat to critical infrastructure has grown to potentially catastrophic dimensions. Critical infrastructure protection has become a matter of national security, public safety, and economic stability. It is imperative the United States Government (USG) examine current responsibilities, develop a comprehensive cybersecurity strategy, cybersecurity regulations, impose standards, and enforce the strongest security measures possible to protect the Nation from cyber attacks to critical infrastructure.

First, this paper will provide a background and definition of what constitutes national critical infrastructure and Critical Infrastructure Protection (CIP). Next, it will discuss the immense vulnerabilities, threats, and risks associated in the protection of critical infrastructure. Finally, it will outline governance and responsibilities of protecting vulnerable infrastructure, culminating with recommendations of which agency should direct and coordinate internet governance and protection to ensure national security, public safety and economic stability.

The Evolving Threat to Critical Infrastructure

The year 2010 served as an alarming wake-up call to the Nation, with the major penetration of the Department of Defense (DOD) classified networks, Google, major

2

Fortune 500 companies, the compromise of the Industrial Control System (ICS) by the cyberweapon Stuxnet worm, the Denial of Service (DOS) attacks over Wikileaks, and exploits against government agencies, companies and consumers.[9] According to Senator Lundgren, "Cyberattacks have grown more frequent, sophisticated, and dangerous." Statics presented in his speech on the Importance of Cybersecurity, showed that from 2009-2011, the Nation experienced a twenty fold increase in cyber attacks; equating to a cyber intrusion every ninety seconds.[10] Other experts agree that, "the problem with cyberattacks has grown to such an extent that some predict an "electronic Waterloo" or an "electronic Pearl Harbor."[11] During a speech to New York City executives in October 2012, Secretary of Defense Leon Panetta warned of the grave dangers present in the cyber domain with the significant escalation of threats. He cited recent examples where cyberattacks to U.S. financial institutions, and oil and energy companies in Saudi Arabia and Qatar caused wide spread internet Denial of Service (DOS); representing the most destructive attacks on the private sector to date. Secretary Panetta cautioned of plausible destructive scenarios where a hybrid of nation state or violent extremist physical and virtual attacks; derailed passenger trains, shut down power grids, and contaminated water supplies, causing destruction and loss of life comparable to the terrorist attacks of 9/11.[12]

During the Cold War, the United States executed limited contingency planning and applied few resources towards threats to infrastructure facilities, which then included key utilities such as power plants and grids, oil and gas pipelines, telecommunications, and critical facilities that affected the continuity of government.[13] Over the last two decades, the nation's leadership has recognized the extraordinary

3

importance of identifying and protecting critical infrastructure. First acknowledged by President Clinton in 1996, then by President Bush in 2001, and most recently by President Obama and Secretary of Defense Panetta; the security of critical infrastructure demands national priority status.

Definition of Critical Infrastructure and Critical Infrastructure Protection

Critical infrastructure is the backbone of the United States dynamic and productive economy. For years, security experts have warned of the extreme vulnerability of the country's banking and telecommunications systems, power and transportation grids, and oil refineries. If shut down, the computer networks that underlie that infrastructure would cause paralysis to daily life.[14]

Legislation regarding cybersecurity of critical infrastructure dates back to 1996, when President Clinton signed Executive Order 13010, which established the President's Commission of Critical Infrastructure. Presidential Decision Directive 63 (PDD 63) followed in May of 1998, requiring the establishment of National capability within five years to protect critical infrastructure from intentional disruption.[15] PDD 63 also directed various federal agencies to lead the government's security efforts. In 2001, Executive Order 13228, signed by President Bush established the office of Homeland Security and the Homeland Security Council. Executive Order 13231 signed eight days later established the President's Critical Infrastructure Protection Board, referring to the importance of information systems to other critical infrastructure such as telecommunications, energy, financial services, manufacturing, water, transportation, health care, and emergency services.[16]

After the terrorist attacks of September 11, 2001, Congress passed the Patriot Act. In that legislation, Congress defined critical infrastructure as "systems and assets, whether physical or virtual, so vital to the United States that the incapacity or destruction of such systems and assets would have a debilitating impact on security, national economic security, national public health or safety, or any combination of those matters."[17] The intent of the Patriot Act serves to "deter and punish terrorist acts, in the United States and around the world, and enhance law enforcement investigatory tools."[18]

Department of Defense tasked the Department of Homeland Security (DHS) with critical infrastructure protection under the Homeland Security Presidential Directive 7 (HSPD 7).[19] HSPD 7 which superseded PDD 63, defines critical infrastructure as "the assets, systems, and networks, whether physical or virtual, so vital to the United States that the incapacitation or destruction would have a debilitating effect on security, national economic security, public health or safety, or any combination thereof."[20] HSPD 7 clarifies executive agency responsibilities for identifying, prioritizing and protecting critical infrastructure.[21] It also establishes U.S. policy for enhancing critical infrastructure protection by establishing a framework for the Department's partners to identify, prioritize, and protect the critical infrastructure in their communities from terrorist attacks.

HSPD 7 identifies 18 critical infrastructure sectors with designated federal Sector Specific Agencies (SSA) to lead protection and resilience building programs and activities. Under HSPD 7, the Department of Homeland Security has the responsibility to identify gaps in existing critical infrastructure sectors.[22] Food and Agriculture, Commercial Facilities, Dams, Energy, Information Technology, Postal and Shipping, Banking and Finance, Communications, the Defense Industrial Base, Government

Facilities, National Monuments and Icons, Transportation Systems, Chemical, Critical Manufacturing, Emergency Services, Healthcare and Public Health, Nuclear Reactors, Materials and Waste, and Water constitute the eighteen Critical Infrastructure Sectors in the United States.[23]

In October 2012, after of years of legislative gridlock, President Obama endorsed Presidential Policy Directive 20 (PDD 20) to establish a national cybersecurity strategy effective enough to counter escalating cyber domain threats. Recently released, the Top Secret directive "effectively authorizes the Department of Defense to adopt a more aggressive, proactive stance on securing the Nation's digital infrastructure." The policy framework also addresses what constitutes offensive and defensive operations, and sets strict standards for authorities to grapple with diverse cybersecurity scenarios. PDD 20 will serve as a decision support tool as national cybersecurity takes on a heightened sense of urgency and new geopolitical implications.[24]

The Internet serves as the nervous system, or the control system for U.S. critical infrastructure, providing hundreds of thousands of interconnected networks, computers, servers, routers, switches and fiber optic cables that enable critical infrastructure to function. The healthy functioning of the information systems supported by the complex interconnected networks remains vital to the nation's security, prosperity, and economy.[25] Critical Infrastructure Protection (CIP) presents a national security and economic imperative. The aggregation of risk and interdependencies posed by the complex, hyper connected core information infrastructure has dramatically increased over the past decade. It is now important to overview the profound vulnerabilities to critical infrastructure operations and the immense threats to the security of critical infrastructure.

Vulnerabilities and Threats to Critical Infrastructure

The globalization, technological complexity, and interdependencies of cyberspace that support critical infrastructure services represent great national opportunity, but also a major source of critical strategic challenges in terms of vulnerabilities and threats. National economic security and prosperity depend on an understanding and strategy for grappling with the multifaceted and incalculable array of cyber vulnerabilities and threats. Sandia National Laboratories cites deficient or nonexistent security governance and administration as the leading causes of critical infrastructure vulnerability. Governance failures include: "failures to adequately define security sensitivities, identify and protect a security perimeter, build comprehensive security through a defense in depth, and to restrict access to data and service to authenticated users based on operational requirements."[26]

Symantec Corporation reports disclose an 81% increase in malicious attack activity, accounting for over 400 million unique variants of malware and an estimated 5.5 billion attacks overall from 2010-2011. In 2011, Symantec identified 4,989 new vulnerabilities, resulting in approximately 95 new vulnerabilities a week during the year.[27] "Lack of governmental control" for critical infrastructure protection represents the most significant national vulnerability. Estimates show that private citizens own and operate 85-90% of critical infrastructure assets.[28] Although, Department of Homeland Security has assigned legal oversight of security for privately owned critical infrastructure, they have no legal authority to set and enforce cybersecurity standards.[29] Protecting the privacy and civil liberties of the American people endowed by current laws and the constitution represents an upmost concern, but also stifles DHS' action and intervention in critical infrastructure protection.[30] According to Jonathan Masters, the expansion of government into private sector security raises a host of issues regarding privacy, innovation and legality.[31]

To exacerbate the complex dilemma, currently, private industry has the responsibility of individually and voluntarily developing and implementing cybersecurity and protection measures for its own assets.[32] While a majority of critical infrastructure companies have boosted cyber defenses and meet security standards, others, lack even basic protection.[33] Without comprehensive control measures, and clear command and control authority to orchestrate government response, the Nation takes an extraordinary risk in relying on private organizations to take individual responsibility and action for protection against foreign governments, criminal syndicates, terrorists, individuals, and state and non-state actors. According to White House reports, these organizations probe and penetrate U.S. financial, energy and public safety systems every day.[34] Established over a decade ago, industry-government partnership represents the cornerstone for national policy. However, in the interest of national security, stronger governmental controls and measures, and tailored cyber defenses remain compulsory.[35]

To further complicate the national critical infrastructure security crisis; "the Federal Government, under DHS, has displayed irresolute and inconsistent leadership concerning cyber critical infrastructure protection," with most of their efforts directed at outreach and awareness activities, rather than development of "robust and comprehensive prevention, response, and reconstitution programs for attacks against critical cyber systems."[36] Additionally, the National Cyber Security Framework Manual for 2012, reports that "within the government alone, it is not unusual for up to a dozen different departments and agencies declare responsibility for national cyber security in various forms, including military, law enforcement, judicial, commerce, infrastructure, interior, intelligence, telecommunications, and other governmental bodies. " Together, this evidence underscores the extraordinary difficulty in integrating organizational efforts to establish coherent action.[37]

Additionally, a vast majority of critical infrastructure owners "have transferred control of their electrical generation and distribution equipment from private, internal networks to Supervisory Control and Data Acquisition (SCADA) systems."[38] Routinely found within power plants, refineries, oil and gas pipelines, chemical and water treatment plants, mining, pharmaceuticals, transportation, manufacturing, and the telecommunications industry;[39] SCADA systems enable users to manage and access systems remotely across Internet Protocol (IP), wireless, and mobile platforms. While this technological advancement has brought greater efficiencies and effectiveness to critical infrastructure management, it has also opened avenues of greater vulnerability for protection.[40]

The highly sophisticated 2010 Stuxnet malware cyberattack provides one of the greatest examples of extraordinary risk presented by SCADA vulnerabilities. Thought to be the first malware specifically targeted at critical infrastructure systems, the offensive cyber weapon exploited four previously unknown zero day vulnerabilities in the Windows operating platform. The worm, transferred via Universal Serial Bus (USB) drive signifies industrial sabotage caused by "physical damage that interferes with critical facility operations or control systems." Sharon Weinberger reported that the Stuxnet malware most likely targeted a uranium enrichment facility in Natanz, Iran. Investigations concluded that the malware code altered the speed of delicate centrifuges causing the machines to spin out of control and fracture, with the main objective of slowing Iran's enrichment capacity, and crippling their nuclear weapons building capabilities.[41] Recent reports cite that Iran successfully defended another round of Stuxnet attacks in the fall of 2012.[42]

According to Senator Lungren, "Stuxnet is a game changer" and "if terrorists or other adversaries were to use the Stuxnet malware to seize control of dams, or chemical and power plants, it could inflict massive death and destruction."[43] Reports indicate the ready availability of the Stuxnet source code over the Internet.[44] This raises concerns that release of the source code information "opened Pandora's box", exposing cyberwarfare blue prints for future attackers. Some believe that the Stuxnet malware source code provided the basis for "study and repurpose" to easily attack Programmable Logic Controllers (PCL) crucial to the operation of critical national infrastructures like traffic systems, power grids, water treatment facilities or any other industrial system that relies on PCLs.[45] David Jeffers of *PC World* reports of two emerging threats, Duqu and Flame, that bear striking resemblance to and apparently evolved from the Stuxnet malware foundation.[46]

The Duqu malware threat, nicknamed "Son of Stuxnet" first surfaced in September 2011. Duqu masks itself, like Stuxnet, as a legitimate code using a driver file signed with a valid digital certificate. Designed to conduct reconnaissance on an Industrial Control System (ICS), such as SCADA; Son of Stuxnet gathers data to

10

conduct future targeted attacks.[47] Considered a sophisticated Trojan, Duqu exploits yet

another Windows zero day vulnerability. Assumed to be much less destructive than

Stuxnet, the Duqu malware threat lacks a destructive payload to damage hardware. The

Trojan collects intelligence with the possible purpose of committing industrial espionage,

blackmail or extortion.[48] Researchers have yet to determine how the malware delivers

data, or what data the malware collected over the year it operated undetected.

After two years in operation, Kaspersky Lab discovered Flame malware in 2011.

Thought to be twenty times more sophisticated than Stuxnet; Flame represents an

advanced cyber espionage attack tool kit. This malware targeted and infected systems

in Iran, Lebanon, Syria, Sudan the Israeli Occupied Territories and other countries in the

Middle East and North Africa. Hosted by a nation state, Flame characterizes "another

tool in the growing arsenal of cyberweaponry" that threatens the security and economic

vitality of national critical infrastructure.[49] In October of 2012, Kaspersky Lab also

uncovered new malware dubbed Mini Flame, which functions independently as a small,

highly flexible malicious program designed to steal data and control infected systems

during targeted cyber espionage operations. Mini Flame malware infected 50-60

systems worldwide, including computers in Lebanon, France, Iran, Lithuania, and the

United States.[50]

The alarming proliferation and replication of Stuxnet, Duqu, Flame, and Mini

Flame that penetrate and establish control over ICS systems has changed the

landscape of targeted cyberattacks, and undermines the underpinnings of the critical

infrastructure backbone. While these malware intrusions require sophisticated code for

execution, they don't require a strong industrial base or well financed operation to

11

uncover ICS vulnerabilities; regularly accomplished by teenagers.[51] Without directed and coordinated prevention and protective efforts, the growing list of vulnerabilities poses unfathomable risk and potential to cause irreparable damage to the Nation.

The Chairman of the Joint Chiefs of Staff, General Dempsey, in a speech to the Commonwealth Club of California referred to cyber as the "Black Swan;" the unknown threat of Nation States and independent actors that terrorize the United States.[52] The Director of National Intelligence's testimony in February 2011, confirmed evidence of dramatic growth in threats to systems supporting critical infrastructure, reporting a more than tripled volume of malicious cyber activity targeting U.S. computers and networks.[53] The dark side to the digital and information revolution enabled by the Internet presents a serious, intrinsically complex, multifaceted and boundary-less collection of threats which include cyberwar, terrorism, crime, espionage, vandalism, and cyber attacks such as Stuxnet, Duqu, Flame, and Mini Flame. The nation faces threats that transcend national boundaries, caused by perpetrators who are relentless, patient, determined, opportunistic, adaptive and flexible.

Along with the 400 million malware variants discovered in 2011 that exposed and potentially exfiltrated personal, confidential and proprietary data; many governments have suffered data breaches, including Australia, Brazil, Canada, India, France, New Zealand, Russia, South Korea, Spain, Turkey, the Netherlands, the United Kingdom, and the United States. Reports indicate that hundreds of private companies suffered significant breaches in 2011-2012, including Citigroup, e-Harmony, Epsilon, Linked-In, the NASDAQ, Sony and Yahoo. One industry reported over 175 million breached records, with an estimated loss of over $125 per record. The Assistant of the

Counterintelligence Division of the Federal Bureau of Investigation (FBI) testified to Congress in 2012, of investigating over $13 billion dollars in losses to the U.S. economy due to economic espionage.[54]

Critical Infrastructure Risks

Managing and mitigating risk in the critical infrastructure arena denotes a shared responsibility among all critical infrastructure stakeholders, including the USG, Department of Defense, Department of Homeland Security, industry partners, non-government organizations, and the private sector. Because the globally interconnected digital information and "communications infrastructure underpin almost every facet of modern society; cybersecurity risks pose some of the most serious economic and national security challenges of the 21st century."[55] According to the Defense Risk Management Framework of the 2010 Quadrennial Defense Review, critical infrastructure protection constitutes an enormous "Operational" risk to the Nation. Exacerbating the fact, the Federal Government has yet to empower DHS with the proper support and authorities to address their responsibility of providing critical infrastructure protection. Additionally, the government has failed to execute Presidential efforts to pass a comprehensive cybersecurity strategy of what should have been the "Cybersecurity Act of 2012, and could have been a first step towards compulsory and sufficient critical infrastructure protection. The Defense Risk Management Framework specifically addresses cyberspace and the fundamental risks posed to operations, personnel, and mission accomplishment as a result of DOD's failure to secure its systems, ensure unfettered access, performance, and resiliency.[56]

The following real world scenarios emphasize the extraordinary risks posed to critical infrastructure by catastrophic utility failures and malicious cyberattacks, which serves to reinforce the insufficiency of current cybersecurity leadership and strategies. The East Coast Blackout of 2003 signifies an unforeseen manmade threat emblematic of the extraordinary risk to national security and economic prosperity. The blackout occurred on August 14, 2003 as a result of a failure to properly maintain power lines in the Ohio Service Area. On this day, a generating plant in Eastlake, Ohio went offline amid a high electrical demand, consequently straining high voltage lines. This series of events caused cascading effects, resulting in the ultimate shutdown of over 100 power plants; with an estimated 50 million customers from the Ontario Province of Canada, and eight states powerless for up to a week. As a result, estimates cite $6-10 million dollars in losses to the United States.[57] Whether by an environmental catastrophe or cyberattack, the sustained loss of power and cascading effects caused by it, could have potentially detrimental economic and life threatening effects for the Nation.

In 2008, the Department of Defense security breach at United States Central Command served as a turning point in National cyber policy for the United States. This pivotal breach represented a foreign nation attack on U.S. classified networks. As a result, the Pentagon made the strategic decision to proclaim cyberspace as a "fifth domain" of warfare, and inaugurated United States Cyber Command (USCYBERCOM) (a sub-unified command) to integrate governmental cyber defenses across the government's "dot.mil" domain.[58] Adding USCYBERCOM to the list of those responsible for security of the nation's critical infrastructure, also adds another layer of complexity to command and control, oversight and authorities in the event of a cyber crisis.

Following the DOD intrusion, in a report commission by The US-China Economic and Security Review Commission, Northrop Grumman revealed that the Chinese People's Liberation Army (PLA) had adopted a formal Information Warfare strategy identified as "Integrated Network Electronic Warfare (INEW)."[59] This strategy forensically linked cyberattacks on Google, Adobe, and 33 other technology and defense firms.[60] Another cyberattack campaign, highlighted in a report to Congress, addressing foreign economic collection and industrial espionage targeted against the United States, code named, "The Night Dragon Campaign" marked the next of many disturbingly sophisticated intrusions on critical infrastructure. In these intrusions, perpetrators launched attacks, collecting commercially sensitive data on oil and gas fields and other sensitive information from energy companies.[61]

In November of 2011, a hacker penetrated a water treatment plant in Houston, Texas gaining access electronically, through the Internet, to their critical SCADA data. The hacker accessed the vital facility to demonstrate ease of entry, and the immense vulnerability of such a critical national asset. There are those foreign governments, criminals, terrorists, and individuals who would and could exploit this vulnerability to endanger the safety, security and prosperity of the United States. The hacker noted that what was most astonishing wasn't the ease with which he accessed the critical system, but the poor response to the serious incident.[62]

In May of 2012, DHS' Industrial Control System Cyber Emergency Response Team (ICS-CERT) uncovered a sophisticated cyber attack; a single campaign behind multiple attempted intrusions into several different pipeline companies in the United States. A Spear Phishing campaign that accompanied the attempted intrusions tipped off the pipeline companies. While the attacker's true motives remain unknown, industry experts suggest that the hackers conducted espionage activities in an attempt to gain control of the gas pipelines to disrupt supplies or access information about gas flows for use in commodities trading. Either way, this intrusion illustrates another remarkable example of the immense vulnerability to infrastructure that is critical to the safety, security and way of life.[63]

Finally, the preceding examples demonstrate the immense vulnerabilities to critical infrastructure and the staggering possibilities for U.S. adversaries, terrorists, and perpetrators capabilities to paralyze the Nation and endanger the security, economic viability, health and the American way of life through destructive action. A White House blog exemplifies this fundamental and preeminent danger in saying:

> In a future conflict, an adversary unable to match our military supremacy on the battlefield might seek to exploit our computer vulnerabilities at home – taking down vital banking systems that could trigger financial crisis – lack of clean water or functioning hospitals could spark a public health emergency, black out, loss of electricity can bring businesses, cites and entire regions to a standstill.[64]

Governance

The Department of Defense, The White House Cybersecurity Coordinator, The Department of Homeland Security, National Security Authority (NSA), Department of Justice (DOJ), the Federal Bureau of Investigation (FBI), the Secret Service, and USCYBERCOM, as well as many other organizations share a major role in the governance and security of critical infrastructure. Cybersecurity responsibilities for critical infrastructure disperse across a wide array of federal departments and agencies, many with overlapping authorities, and none with sufficient decision authority to direct actions to mitigate conflicting issues in a consistent way. According to the 2009

Cyberspace Policy Review, over the past 15 years, the Nation's approach to cybersecurity has failed to keep pace with emerging cyber threat."[65] Additionally, organization of the U.S. Federal governmental efforts unsuccessfully addresses the evolving problem.

Homeland Security Policy Directive 7 (HSPD 7) assigns DOD the primary responsibility of Critical Infrastructure Identification, Prioritization, and Protection. DOD, under the advisement of the Assistant Secretary of Defense (ASD) for Homeland Defense and Americas' Security Affairs ASD (HD&ASA), maintains two roles in the protection of critical infrastructure; as a Federal department, and as the Sector Specific Agency for the Defense Industrial Base. The ASD (HD&ASA) leads national efforts, providing policy, guidance, oversight, and resource advocacy for the two assigned DOD roles. HSPD 7 also directs national level collaboration to "prevent, deter and mitigate the effects of deliberate efforts to destroy, incapacitate, or exploit" critical infrastructure.[66] Within DOD, seven different agencies, each with distinct characteristics and operating models, share responsibility for Critical Infrastructure Specific Sectors. Agencies include: the Department of Agriculture, Human and Health Service, the Environmental Protection Agency, and the Departments of Energy, Treasury, Interior and Defense.[67]

In 2009, President Obama announced a new White House Cybersecurity Coordinator position charged with the important responsibility of orchestrating cybersecurity across the whole of government.[68] The White House Cybersecurity Coordinator advises on a wide array of cybersecurity issues to include cyber defense, federal security policies, and online privacy and civil liberties. He or she serves as the administrator for unified policy and voice for the White House and USG. Unfortunately, even though the Cyber Coordinator has regular access to influence the President, the National Security Staff, and the National Economic Council, he or she wields no authority to compel action or direct national efforts in the event of a major cybersecurity breach or crisis. The position also lacks congressional oversight and budgetary authority, depicting grave shortfalls in the validity of the position.

DOD, under HSPD 7, tasked the Department of Homeland Security with the extraordinary task of critical infrastructure protection. DHS conducts this mission without a national comprehensive and authoritative cybersecurity strategy. Protection of critical infrastructure accounts for one of twenty two, highly sophisticated, rigorous Homeland Security tasks that the Department of Homeland Security executes; ranging from securing the nation's borders, securing the nation from terrorism to national disaster. Considered the third largest cabinet department in DOD, DHS employs over 240,000 people. The sheer complexity of DHS and its missions, to include cybersecurity, contributes to cabinet shortfalls to achieve measurable results in critical infrastructure protection. Additionally, the FBI and Secret Service work in conjunction with DHS investigating, predicting, preventing, detecting, and responding to cyber incidents.

In 2010, DOD and DHS signed a cybersecurity pact to formalize cooperation between the two agencies; enabling DHS to capitalize on the National Security Agency's (NSA) advanced technical expertise in signal intelligence and cryptologic work.[69] "A recent agreement embeds Department of Defense cyber analysts within DHS to support the National Cybersecurity and Communications Integration Center (NCCIC), and provisions a full-time senior DHS leader to NSA, along with a support team comprised of DHS privacy, civil liberties and legal personnel.[70] Additionally, DOD, DHS and NSA work collaboratively to protect critical infrastructure as part of the National Cyber Investigative Joint Task Force.[71]

The Department of Justice (DOJ), in partnership with USCYBERCOM also plays crucial roles in cybersecurity. The DOJ execute their role in the threat reduction and attribution by "identifying cyber offenders, seizing their hardware and assets, and deterring their conduct through arrest and appropriately severe punishment."[72] USCYBERCOM, a sub-unified command under United States Strategic Command (US-STRATCOM), responsibilities include comprehensive defense of the Department of Defense information networks, and when directed, execution of full spectrum cyberspace operations to ensure the United States their allies freedom of action in cyberspace, while denying the adversaries the same.[73]

United States Codes Title 6 (Homeland Security), Title 10 (Military) and Title 50 (Intelligence) also play a role in governance of critical infrastructure. These laws establish jurisdictions, guidelines and restrictions for the involvement of Department of Defense resources in the protection of privately owned critical infrastructure. They limit the Department of Homeland Security's response and authority to critical infrastructure security breaches. Updating this legislation to meet national and global cybersecurity threats presents another enormous, but necessary challenge.[74]

It's clear that a coordinated effort on behalf of these agencies without executive oversight and authority lends itself to considerable difficulty in coherent action; with multiple owners and donors to the critical infrastructure cybersecurity process. The USG must integrate the competing interests of all stakeholders to derive a holistic vision and strategy which adequately addresses cybersecurity related issues confronting the United States. The Nation must also develop the policies, processes, people, and technology required to mitigate cybersecurity related risks.[75]

Recommendations

In an era of turbulence and national fiscal austerity, the United States can no longer accept the level of national security and economic risk posed by the absence of an integrated, comprehensive national cybersecurity strategy, vague policies, outdated legislation, and lack of coherent government action. The President has already taken the first step towards grappling with these complex cybersecurity issues by instituting the White House Cybersecurity Coordinator position. However, this position requires authority delegation by the President to "oversee both civilian and military cybersecurity efforts, direct subordinate agency action, maintain formal tasking authority, adjust priorities, and the power to allocate resources and make budgetary changes" based on the operational environment.[76] Recommended as a political appointee position, the Coordinator would maintain responsibility for congressional accountability and consent of federal cybersecurity efforts.

Restructuring the White House Cybersecurity Coordinator responsibilities provides one authoritative and properly empowered Executive Agent (EA) for coordination of all national cybersecurity efforts, to prevent or prepare for catastrophic cyber consequences. Having one EA will enable the Coordinator to identify tensions, fault lines and seams, share critical threat information, and integrate military efforts when necessary.[77] It serves to synchronize and align all legislative, policy, operational, functional, security, research and development, criminal, and international efforts in a coordinated and fiscally responsible manner and direction, thus providing programmatic focus and direction, while drastically reducing federal duplication of effort and cost. This concept implements DOD's End to End (E2E) philosophy,[78] which advocates eliminating middle layers and steps to optimize process performance and efficiency. Another advantage to adapting the current White House Cybersecurity Coordinator responsibilities and authority includes direct access to influence the President, the National Security Council, and the National Economic Council to "build cross organizational consensus within the executive branch."[79] Overcoming parochialisms and paralyzing bureaucracy presents one the greatest rewards and challenges of this proposal. This proposal, if not fully implemented as recommended, falls short of gaining the necessary traction to implement required changes to counter emergent cyber threats to critical infrastructure.

Unconventional threats pose the most likely and dangerous security challenges the Nation faces.[80] The adversary has shown the operational competence and tenacity to damage and disrupt the nation with lethal force through cyberattacks. Failure by DOD to secure cyberspace poses a vital risk and unacceptable cost to the security and ability of the Nation to accomplish its defense missions.[81] The likelihood of profound and catastrophic cyber consequences continues to grow and threatens U.S. national interests. Properly empowering the White House Cybersecurity Coordinator with authority provides the greatest approach and opportunity to reducing risk. The magnitude and immediacy of risk posed by cyber threats to U.S. interest requires directed effort and authority to detect, assess, manage and mitigate risk while coordinating cyber protective measures to protect and advance the Nation's interests. The White House Cybersecurity Coordinator must have authority to implement federal risk-based standards to minimize threats, and the agility to adapt rapidly, and respond appropriately to the imminent and credible cyber threats to the Nation.[82]

The second recommendation in tackling the extraordinary cybersecurity challenge resides in enacting the appropriate legislation to empower the Department of Homeland Security to manage and protect privately owned critical infrastructure. Endorsing legislation to empower DHS to direct and enforce the protection of privately owned and managed national critical infrastructure threatens American privacy and civil liberties, however the extraordinary risks posed by inaction remains a threat to the integrity, security, and posture of national critical infrastructure. DHS has built strong relationships and recognized minor successes in implementation of the industry-government partnership policy, which falls woefully short of fully protecting the Nation's critical infrastructure. The USG must empower DHS to set and enforce minimum security standards for private critical infrastructure owners and managers to mitigate vulnerabilities and threats to the Nation.

Current cybersecurity regulatory requirements fail to sufficiently address the immediate risk posed by an invisible, fearless and tenacious adversary. Failure to address persistent gaps in critical infrastructure protection represents one of the greatest threats to national safety and security. The temporary or permanent catastrophic loss of power to the nation, hospitals, critical care facilities, and emergency services, access to water, dams, DOD networks, and to sensitive and classified information, threaten loss of life and would devastate national defense capabilities.[83] While President Obama's new Executive Order – Improving Critical Infrastructure Cybersecurity and Presidential Policy Directive 20 provide a step in the right direction in acknowledging critical infrastructure cybersecurity gaps, they fall short of generating proper cybersecurity protection measures.[84] It's clear that critical infrastructure owners and managers will continue to forgo the extra effort and costs to meet currently defined cybersecurity specifications if not strictly monitored and enforced with legal and financial repercussions.[85] Therefore, DOD must immediately empower DHS to raise the cybersecurity baseline to properly protect the Nation's critical infrastructure.

Conclusion

Previous examples have illustrated how easily perpetrators penetrate and exploit national and private cybersecurity defenses. The potential disruption or destruction of critical infrastructure could cost hundreds of billions of dollars, lead to hundreds of thousands of deaths, threaten the safety, security and health of American citizens, demolish the U.S. economy, cause widespread public fear and panic, and dismantle the United States as a world leader.[86] The United States can't wait for a catastrophe to take action; it must take immediate and proactive measures now, by adequately empowering the White House Cybersecurity Coordinator and enacting legislation to counter the prolific threat to national security posed by cybersecurity threats to critical infrastructure.

This paper successfully discussed what constitutes national critical infrastructure, critical infrastructure protection, the extraordinary vulnerabilities, and threats inherent in the protection of critical infrastructure, as well as critical infrastructure authorities and governance, with the objective of identifying the imminent national risks inherent in current critical infrastructure cybersecurity structure and policies, and proposing changes necessary to counter the dangerous and imminent risks.

Cybersecurity for critical infrastructure must become a national priority. The USG must adapt to address the complex global network where connectivity, speed, and capacity create new possibilities for economic prosperity and national security.[87] The

USG must empower the Department of Homeland Security with appropriate authorities,

and most importantly establish an executive agent to direct the Nation's effort in the

intrinsically complex and paramount task of protecting national critical infrastructure.[88]

Failing to implement these necessary measures, and to acknowledge the highly

destructive and escalating threats to critical infrastructure places the Nation in great

peril resulting in absolutely devastating consequences.

Endnotes

[1] "Cybersecurity," linked from *The White House Home Page* at "National Security Council," http://www.whitehouse.gov/cybersecurity (accessed February 19, 2013).

[2] Alexander Klimburg, *National Cyber Security Framework Manual* (Tallinn, Estonia: NATO Cooperative Cyber Defense Center of Excellence, 2012), http://www.ccdoe.org/369.htm (accessed December 13, 2012), 4.

[3] Ibid., 556.

[4] Franklin D. Kramer, Stuart H. Starr, and Larry Wentz, *Cyberpower and National Security* (Washington D.C.: Potomac Books, Inc., 2009), 543.

[5] Ibid.

[6] "The Comprehensive National Cyber Security Initiative," linked from *The White House Home Page* at "National Security Council," "http://www.whitehouse.gov/cybersecurity/comprehensive-national-cybersecurity-initiative (accessed November 19, 2012).

[7] "The National Strategy for the Physical Protection of Critical Infrastructures and Key Assets," February 2003, http://www.dhs.gov/national-strategy-physical-protection-critical-infrastructure-and-key-assets (accessed October 12, 2012).

[8] Center for Strategic and International Studies, *Cybersecurity Two Years Later*, Washington, DC: CSIS, 2011), http://csis.org/publication/cybersecurity-two-years-later (accessed October 3, 2012).

[9] Ibid., 1.

[10] "Lungren Speech Highlights the Importance of Cybersecurity," *Federal Information & News Dispatch, Inc.*, in Proquest http://search.proquest.com/docview/1034715675?accountid=4444 (accessed October 4, 2012).

24

[11] Anthoney H. Cordesman, and Justin G. Cordesman, *Cyber-Threats, Information Warfare, and Critical Infrastructure Protection* (Westport, Connecticut: Praeger, 2003), 2.

[12] "Remarks by Secretary Panetta on Cybersecurity to the Business Executives for National Security, New York City," October 11, 2012, linked from *United States Department of Defense Home Page* at "Office of the Assistant Secretary of Defense (Public Affairs)," http://www.defense.gov/transcrips/transcript.aspx?transcriptid=5136 (accessed January 29, 2013).

[13] Ibid., 3.

[14] Tom Gjelten, "U.S. Outlines Cybersecurity Initiative," May 12, 2011, http://www.npr.org/2011/05/12/136250408/obama-lays-out-cybersecurity-plan (accessed October 4, 2012)

[15] "Presidential Decision Directive/NSC-63," May 22, 1998, http://www.fas.org/irp/offdocs/pdd/pdd-63.htm (accessed October 12, 2012).

[16] John Moteff and Paul Parformak, *Critical Infrastructure and Key Asset Definition and Identification* (Washington, DC: U.S. Library of Congress, Congressional Research Service, October 1, 2004), 9, http://www.fas.org/sgp/crs/RL32631.pdf (accessed October 12, 2012).

[17] "USA Patriot Act," October 26, 2001, http://www.gpo.gov/fdsys/pkg/PLAW-107publ56/html/PLAW-107publ56.htm (accessed December 13, 2012).

[18] John Moteff and Paul Parformak, *Critical Infrastructure and Key Asset Definition and Identification*, 9.

[19] "Critical Infrastructure Sectors," linked from *Department of Homeland Security Home Page* at "Critical Infrastructure Sectors," http://www.dhs.gov/critical-infrastructure-sectors (accessed November 12, 2012).

[20] Ibid.

[21] John Moteff and Paul Parformak, *Critical Infrastructure and Key Asset Definition and Identification*, 12.

[22] "Critical Infrastructure Sectors."

[23] Ibid.

[24] "Obama Directive Endorses Offensive Cyber Capabilities," *Simple Security Online*, November 19, 2012, http://www.simplysecurity.com/2012/11/19/obama-directive-endorses-offensive-cyber-capabilities/ (accessed February 2, 2013).

[25] "National Strategy to Secure Cyberspace," linked from *Department of Homeland Security Home Page* at "National Strategy to Secure Cyberspace," http://www.dhs.gov/national-strategy-secure-cyberspace (accessed October 8, 2012).

[26] Jason Stamp, John Dillenger, and William Young, "Common Vulnerabilities in Critical Infrastructure Control Systems," May 22, 2003, http://scholar.google.com/scholar_url?hl=en&q=http://citeseerx.ist.psu.edu/viewdoc/download%3Fdoi%3D10.1.1.172.1908%26rep%3Drep1%26type%3Dpdf&sa=X&scisig=AAGBfm0WZbC_ro8JeAfrSRU9GZga0Sg0hA&oi=scholarr (accessed January 29, 2013).

[27] Symantec Corporation, "Internet Security Threat Report 2011," (Mountain View, CA: Symantec Corp, 2012), http://www.symantec.com/threatreport.html (accessed October 8, 2012).

[28] Critical Infrastructure, "Long-term Trends and Drivers and Their Implications for Emergency Management," June 2011, http://www.fema.gov/pdf/about/programs/oppa/critical_infrastructure_paper.pdf (accessed January 2, 2012); Tom Gjelten, "U.S. Outlines Cybersecurity Initiative," May 12, 2011, http://www.npr.org/2011/05/12/136250408/obama-lays-out-cybersecurity-plan (accessed October 4, 2012).

[29] Ibid.

[30] "Taking the Cyberattack Threat Seriously," *The White House Blog,* entry posted July 20, 2012, http://www.whitehouse.gov/blog/2012/07/23/taking-cyberattack-threat-seriously (accessed October 2012).

[31] Jonathan Masters, "Confronting the Cyber Threat" *Council on Foreign Relations Online,* May 23, 2011, http://www.cfr.org/technology-and-foreign-policy/confronting-cyber-threat/p15577 (accessed October 12, 2013).

[32] "Lungren Speech Highlights the Importance of Cybersecurity."

[33] "Taking the Cyberattack Threat Seriously."

[34] Ibid.

[35] Scott Algeier, "The Cybersecurity Cornerstone," *The Center for Infrastructure Protection, no. 10 (2012): 10,* http://cip.gmu.edu/the-cip-report (accessed December 29, 2012).

[36] Kramer, Starr, and Wentz, *Cyberpower and National Security,* 543.

[37] Alexander Klimburg, *National Cyber Security Framework Manual,* 30.

[38] Justin Blum, "Hackers Target U.S. Power Grid," *The Washington Post Online,* March 11, 2005, http://www.washingtonpost.com/wp-dyn/articles/A25738-2005Mar10.html (accessed October 12, 2012).

[39] Jean Thilmany, "Scada Security?" *Mechanical Engineering Online* 134, no. 6 (June 2012): 26-31, in ProQuest, http://search.proquest.com/docview/1021400449?accountid=4444 (accessed October 12, 2012).

[40] McAfee, "Protecting Critical Infrastructure," http://www.mcafee.com/us/resources/solution-briefs/sb-critical-infrastructure-protect.pdf (accessed October 10, 2012).

[41] Sharon Weinberger, "Is This the Start of Cyberwarfare?" *Nature Online* 474, no. 7350 (June 9, 2011): 142-145, in ProQuest, http://search.proquest.com/docview/872363390?accountid=4444 (accessed November 5, 2012).

[42] Natalie Weinstein, "Stuxnet Attacks Iran Again, Reports Say," *CNET Review Online*, December 25, 2012, http://news.cnet.com/8301-1009_3-57560799-83/stuxnet-attacks-iran-again-reports-say (accessed January 29, 2013).

[43] "Lungren Speech Highlights the Importance of Cybersecurity."

[44] Thomas Ricker, "Stuxnet Source Code Could Open a Pandora's Box of Cyberwarfare," March 5, 2012, http://www.theverge.com/2012/3/5/2845848/stuxnet-source-code-opens-a-pandoras-box-of-cyberwarfare (accessed November 19, 2012).

[45] Ibid.

[46] David Jeffers, "The Pandora's Box of Stuxnet, Duqu, and Flame," *PC World Online*, June 1, 2012, http://www.pcworld.com/article/256643/the_pandoras_box_of_stuxnet_duqu_and_flame.html (accessed December 30, 2012).

[47] Kim Zetter, "Son of Stuxnet Found in The Wild on Systems in Europe," October 18, 2011, http://www.wired.com/threatlevel/2011/10/son-of-stuxnet-in-the-wild/ (accessed December 30, 2012).

[48] "Duqu: Steal Everything," http://www.kaspersky.com/about/press/duqu (accessed January 29, 2013).

[49] Kim Zetter, "Meet Flame, the Massive Spy Malware Infiltrating Iranian Computers," May 28, 2012, http://www.wired.com/threatlevel/2012/05/flame/all.html (accessed December 30, 2012).

[50] "This New 'Mini-Flame' Virus is Sweeping Through the Middle East," *Business Insider Online*, October 15, 2012, http://www.businessinsider.com/this-new-flame-virus-is-sweeping-through-the-middle-east.html (accessed December 31, 2012).

[51] Alexander Klimburg, *National Cyber Security Framework Manual*, 7.

[52] "Martin Dempsey: Cyber Attacks are Black Swan Threat to US," August 2, 2012, YouTube, video file. http://www.youtube.com/watch?v=aDAG1dJNu4Q (accessed January 2, 2013).

[53] U.S. Government Accountability Office, *Critical Infrastructure Protection: Cybersecurity Guidance is Available, but More Can Be Done to Promote its Use: Report to Congressional Requesters* (Washington, DC: U.S. Government Accountability Office, December 2011).

[54] Alexander Klimburg, *National Cyber Security Framework Manual*, 6.

[55] "Cyberspace Policy Review: Assuring a Trusted and Resilient Information and Communications Infrastructure."

http://www.whitehouse.gov/assets/documents/Cyberspace_Policy_Review_final.pdf (accessed October 18, 2012).

[56] "Section VI: A Defense Risk Management Framework," *Defense News Online*, January 27, 2010, http://www.defensenews.com/article/20100127/DEFSECT04/1270309/SECTION-VI-DEFENSE-RISK-MANAGEMENT-FRAMEWORK (accessed November 5, 2012).

[57] "Northeast Blackout of 2003," *The Energy Library Online*, August 13, 2003, http://theenergylibrary.com/node/13088 (accessed January 2, 2012).

[58] Jonathan Masters, "Confronting the Cyber Threat."

[59] Brian Krekel, "Capability of the People's Republic of China to Conduct Cyber Warfare and Computer Network Exploitation," October 9, 2009, http://www.uscc.gov/researchpapers/2009/NorthropGrumman_PRC_Cyber_Paper_FINAL_Approved%20Report_16Oct2009.pdf (accessed December 30, 2012).

[60] John E. Dunn, "Google Hack Hit 33 Other Companies," *Techworld Online*, January 13, 2010, http://blogs.techworld.com/war-on-error/2010/01/who-is-to-blame-for-the-google-hack-everyone/index.htm (accessed January 1, 2013).

[61] John E. Dunn, "Chinese Accused of Huge 'Night Dragon' Attack in Energy Sector," *Techworld Online*, February 10, 2011, http://news.techworld.com/security/3260379/chinese-accused-of-huge-night-dragon-attack-on-energy-sector/ (accessed January 1, 2013).

[62] Matt Liebowitz, "Hacker Says He Breached Texas' Water Treatment Control Plant," *Security News Daily Online*, November 21, 2011, http://www.technewsdaily.com/7335-hacker-texas-water-plant.html (accessed January 1, 2013).

[63] Ed Crooks, "Hackers Target U.S. Natural Gas Pipelines," *FT.COM Online*, May 8, 2012, http://www.ft.com/intl/cms/s/0/36a4e4b0-9927-11e1-9a57-00144feabdc0.html (accessed January 2, 2013).

[64] "Taking the Cyberattack Threat Seriously."

[65] "Cyberspace Policy Review: Assuring a Trusted and Resilient Information and Communications Infrastructure."

[66] "Roles and Responsibilities," linked from *Department of Defense Home Page* at "Assistant Secretary of Defense for Homeland Defense and Americas' Security Affairs," http://policy.defense.gov/OUSDPOffices/ASDforHomelandDefenseAmericasSecurityAffa/DefenseCriticalInfrastructureProgram/Roles.aspx (accessed December 31, 2012).

[67] "Homeland Security Presidential Directive 7: Critical Infrastructure Identification, Prioritization, and Protection," linked from *Department of Homeland Security Home Page* at "Homeland Security," http://www.dhs.gov/homeland-security-presidential-directive-7 (accessed December 31, 2012).

[68] "Introducing the New Cybersecurity Coordinator," *The White House Blog*, entry posted December 22, 2009, http://www.whitehouse.gov/blog/2009/12/22/introducing-new-cybersecurity-coordinator (accessed December 12, 2012).

[69] Jonathan Masters, "Confronting the Cyber Threat," 6.

[70] Mark Rockwell, "Napolitano Doesn't See Conflicts in Cyber-Security Arrangement," *Government Security News Online*, October 29, 2010, http://www.gsnmagazine.com/article/21735/napolitano_doesn%E2%80%99t_see_conflicts_cyber_security_ar (accessed January 3, 2013).

[71] "National Cyber Investigative Task Force," linked from *The Federal Bureau of Investigation Home Page* at "Cyber Crime," http://www.fbi.gov/about-us/investigate/cyber/ncijtf (accessed December 14, 2012).

[72] "Deputy Attorney General James M. Cole Speaks at the GSK Press Conference," April 12, 2011, linked from *The United States Department of Justice Home Page* at "Justice News," http://www.justice.gov/iso/opa/dag/speeches/2012/dag-speech-1207021.html (accessed January 4, 2013).

[73] "United States Cyber Command," linked from *United States Strategic Command Home Page* at "United States Cyber Command," http://www.stratcom.mil/factsheets/Cyber_Command.html (accessed December 12, 2012).

[74] "McCain Wants Special Cybersecurity Panel," *Blackfive Online*, July 16, 2011, http://www.blackfive.net/main/2011/07/mccain-wants-special-cyber-security-panel.html (accessed February 2, 2013).

[75] Ibid.

[76] Kevin P. Newmeyer, "Who Should Lead U.S. Cybersecurity Efforts?" *Prism Online* (Washington, DC: National Defense University Press, March, 2012), 118-126, http://www.ndu.edu/press/lib/pdf/prism3-2/prism3-2.pdf (accessed October 10, 2012).

[77] Tessa Gellerson and Katie Breitbach, 2009, "Turf Wars Predicted for the New Cybersecurity Czar," *National Defense Online* 94, no. 669: 15, in ProQuest, http://search.proquest.com/docview/213311517?accountid=4444 (accessed February 2, 2013).

[78] "Definition: End to End," http://www.investopedia.com/terms/e/end-to-end.asp#ixzz26vxfxMoM (accessed February 11, 2013).

[79] Ibid., 123.

[80] Nathal P. Freier, "Toward a Risk Management Defense Strategy," *Strategic Studies Institute Online*, August 2009, http://www.strategicstudiesinstitute.army.mil/pubs/summary.cfm?q=934 (accessed February 19, 2013).

[81] "Section VI: A Defense Risk Management Framework."

[82] U.S. Government Printing Office, *The Future of the U.S. Military Ten Years After 9/11 and the Consequences of Defense Sequestration: Report to Committee on Armed Services of the House of Representatives* (Washington, DC: U.S. Government Printing Office, November 2011), http://www.gpo.gov/fdsys/pkg/CPRT-112HPRT71102/html/CPRT-112HPRT71102.htm (accessed February 19, 2013).

[83] U.S. Government Accountability Office, *Cybersecurity: Report to Congressional Addressees* (Washington, DC: U.S. Government Accountability Office, February 14, 2013).

[84] "Executive Order - Improving Critical Infrastructure Cybersecurity," February 12, 2013, linked from The White House Home Page at "Executive Order – Improving Critical Infrastructure Cybersecurity," http://www.whitehouse.gov/the-press-office/2013/02/12/executive-order-improving-critical-infrastructure-cybersecurity (accessed February 14, 2013); "Obama's Directive Endorses Offensive Cyber Capabilities," *Simple Security Online*, November 19, 2012, http://www.simplysecurity.com/2012/11/19/obama-directive-endorses-offensive-cyber-capabilities/ (accessed February 14, 2013).

[85] U.S. Government Accountability Office, *Cybersecurity: Report to Congressional Addressees*, 42.

[86] Brian Wingfield and Jeff Bliss, "Thousands Seen Dying if Terrorists Attack U.S. Power Grid," *Bloomberg Online*, November 14, 2012, http://www.bloomberg.com/news/2012-11-14/thousands-seen-dying-if-terrorists-attack-vulnerable-u-s-grid.html (accessed November 19, 2012).

[87] "Cybersecurity Two Years Later, 3."

[88] Ibid., 7.

www.ingramcontent.com/pod-product-compliance
Lightning Source LLC
Chambersburg PA
CBHW080751290526
45790CB00008B/3400